Amazing Grace

A short collection of Christian verse

Megan Carter

TSL Publications

First published in Great Britain in 2018
By TSL Publications, Rickmansworth

Copyright © 2018 Megan Carter

ISBN / 978-1-912416-59-2

The right of Megan Carter to be identified as the author of this work has been asserted by the author in accordance with the UK Copyright, Designs and Patents Act 1988.

All rights reserved. No part of this publication may be reproduced, stored in a retrieval system or transmitted, in any form or by any means without the prior written permission of the publisher, nor be otherwise circulated in any form of binding or cover other than that in which it is published and without a similar condition being imposed on the subsequent buyer.

Font: Black Chancery by Doug Miles

Commendation

As you will see from these poems, Megan's Christian faith is rooted in a real delight in Christ and His Word. As I've read through these poems I have been reminded of some that have been inspired from All Souls sermons. I was delighted to see how they had dropped into Megan's heart and found their way into her work.

My favourite poem is entitled 'The British Museum' which views the historicity of some of the Biblical material, and it is wonderful to have what we see so creatively summarised and described.

I'm delighted to commend this volume to you, and hope it will lift your heart, as it lifted mine.

Rico Tice
Senior Minister
All Souls, Langham Place

Dedicated to the memory
of our son David,
whose life was short but
gave us such joy.

Without him this book would never
have been written.

Contents

Creation	9
The chief purpose of man	10
The day the sun stood still	11
Queen of Sheba	12
Samson	13
Life, death, the universe and everything	14
Samuel	15
Joshua	16
History in the making	17
Tour of the British Museum	18
The British Museum	19
God's handwriting	20
Creation/fall/redemption/glory	21
The stranger	22
The Christmas message	23
John the Baptist	24
Meals with Jesus	25
The water of life	26
Thy kingdom come	27
An equestrian tale	28
The I am	29
The crossroad	30
The travellers	31
Prove it	32
Paul the man of God	33
Name above all names	34
The reformation	35
We remember	36
But who do you say I am?	37
Ring out the bells	38
Acknowledgements	39
Megan	40

Creation

Sun that moves at the Master's word
Moon that lowers her gaze,
Tides that ebb and flow for Him
And nights that turn to days.

The starry host in heaven above
Too numerous to see,
Their orbits and their circuits run
Obeying His decree

All creation praises Him
The wind and waves are calmed,
At His voice 'Peace, be still'
They bend to His command.

But what of man who stands alone
Amidst such grand display,
He turns his head, ignores his Lord
And blindly walks away.

All creation stands aghast
Too dreadful to behold,
That man should turn his back on God
And sin should takes its hold.

The mysteries of God are vast
Who ever could devise
A plan for man's redemption
Where a saviour comes and dies?

'A body prepared to do Thy will
Not mine but Thine be done',
On beams of wood raised up to die
A mighty battle won.

The way is made, the curtain torn
No longer gripped in sin,
The Maker makes a way for man
Who hid his face from Him.

And now to Him who made all things
Let all creation sing,
Your kingdom come, Your will be done
Our great Redeemer King.

The chief purpose of man

How clever man is, he has conquered the skies,
Reached for the stars and stepped onto the moon,
But he still does not know why he is here
Or what is the purpose, or why he was born.

And did it all start with one big bang
As stars and galaxies burst into space?
Or was it the hand of a mighty Creator
Who lovingly fashioned this wondrous place?

Into this world God planted a garden
And placed man there to enjoy its delights,
But he soon disobeyed and sin entered in,
And so man was banished and thrust from God's sight.

How gracious God is, He has reached out again
To reconcile man and bring him back home,
Sin's debt has been paid by the death of His Son,
To know God as Father is why man was born.

(Westminster Shorter Catechism
What is the chief end of man?
A man's chief end is to glorify God and enjoy Him forever.)

The day the sun stood still

Joshua prayed as entrenched in battle,
He called on his God to come to his aid
For the sun to stand still and the moon to rest,
And as God responded the sun was stayed.

The battle was waged and the enemy routed,
The night held back making victory theirs,
For God had extended his mighty arm
As the day was lengthened in answer to prayer.

Another battle had yet to be fought,
No sun just darkness covered the land,
A cross was erected, a Man nailed upon it,
Jesus our Saviour dying for man.

He came as the Light stepping into our darkness,
Spreading hope where once there was none
Forgiveness, salvation is ours, will we take it?
This wonderful gift bestowed by God's Son.

Queen of Sheba

She came from afar with a great retinue
Her caravan laden with spices and gold,
Solomon's fame had spread to her kingdom
She had many hard questions she wished to unfold.

When she witnessed his splendour, his house and his servants,
The favour of God that had made him a king,
She could not believe it, until she had seen it,
This king blessed by God with every good thing.

King Solomon answered all of her questions,
Amazed at his wisdom and riches and gold,
The queen praised his God who had blessed him so greatly,
She told him 'the half has never been told'.

And so with our God and mighty Creator,
As our minds try to fathom his great Majesty,
Not even the half can we understand now
But we shall when we meet in Eternity.

(The Lord Jesus said: 'The Queen of Sheba came from a distant land to hear the wisdom of Solomon: and behold a greater than Solomon is here'. (Matthew 12v.42))

Samson

Disobedient Israel, crushed by her foes
Cries out to God and Samson is born,
No razor is ever to touch his head,
His hair growing long, never cut or shorn.

The strong man of the Bible, a Nazirite from birth
As judge and deliverer he's sent by the Lord,
Blessed by his God with unparalled strength
To rescue Israel from the Philistine horde.

The Philistine nation is under attack
And Samson's great strength brings fear all around,
As Israel's deliverer he could not be stopped,
His fierceness and vengeance knowing no bounds

Samson now falls for a Philistine woman
Her name is Delilah, she plans his downfall,
Desperate to know the source of his strength
They bribe her with silver and she tells them all.

If you shave off his hair his strength will be gone,
He'll be just like a man with no extra might,
So while on Delilah's lap he lies sleeping
They cut off his hair and then bind him tight.

They gouge out his eyes and take him to Gaza,
They put him in prison to grind out the corn,
But while in the prison his hair begins growing,
God restoring his power on the locks that were shorn.

A great sacrifice is arranged in the temple
They call out for Samson to watch him perform
Samson cries to his God to avenge his tormentors
And prays for the strength they all thought had gone.

His hands find the pillars and pushes them outwards,
In such a disaster none would survive,
Crushing himself and the Philistines with him
Killing more in his death than he did when alive.

(In his death Samson killed more Philistines than during his lifetime. **The Lord Jesus in his death killed death itself.**)

Life, death, the universe and everything

It was in the garden when man first met
His Creator God and walked with Him,
The pleasures of Eden were his to enjoy
The genesis of man who was then without sin.

To make him complete God took Adam's rib
Forming Eve to be by his side,
But the devil appeared in the form of a snake
Offering fruit that they should have declined.

Paradise lost, they were sent from that place,
They had disobeyed God and death entered in,
No longer to walk in the cool of the day
And enjoy all the pleasures that God could bring.

But God's in control of all He has made,
Our world and beyond and mysteries untold,
There are more things in heaven and earth than we know
To be revealed as time ends and eternity unfolds.

Samuel
(or two women in the kitchen)

Penninah and Hannah both wed to one man,
Peninnah had children but Hannah had none
Hannah provoked by the other wife
Cried out to God to give her a son.

God hears Hannah's cry, an answer is given,
Asked of the LORD Samuel is born
In the temple with Eli ministering daily
She gives back her son, as she had sworn.

The two sons of Eli corrupted the priesthood,
The Word of the LORD for long had been still.
Now God turns to Samuel, who answers the call,
'Here I am LORD to do thy will'.

Throughout the land Samuel was known,
From Dan to Beersheba went forth his fame,
But what do we know of Penninah's children?
Nothing at all, not even a name.

In Samuel we see a glimpse of the Saviour,
Both children of promise fulfilling God's plan,
Samuel restoring the nation of Israel,
The Saviour bring salvation to man.

Joshua

Joshua sent them to spy out the land,
The two men arrived at Rahab's door
She took them inside and hid them there
This time would be different, not as before.

Their fathers had wandered for forty years,
Not even Moses had entered the land,
They could not believe God was true to His word,
They could not rely on His mighty hand.

But God was the God of the second chance
And now they were ready to take Jericho,
With trumpets and shouting and marching around
The walls fell down without striking a blow.

A scarlet thread Rahab hung from her window
This was the sign and part of the plan
That all of her family would be saved
As Joshua's troops invaded the land

The scarlet thread links us to the cross
Its redemptive power the years have spanned,
And just like Rahab we have been saved -
We too will enter the Promised Land.

History in the making

The king had a dream and called for his wise men
But none could interpret what the dream meant,
Only Daniel could give him an answer
And tell the king of the unfolding events.

The statue he dreamed of depicted four kingdoms,
King Nebuchadnezzar was the head made of gold
But each of these kingdoms would all be demolished
This mystery to Daniel God had foretold.

A rock cut out not by human hands
Would smash the statue and break it down
And the rock would become like a mighty mountain
Filling the earth and all around.

Today as we see new kingdoms arising,
Dangerous and evil, filled with hate,
They too will fall and be broken in pieces
Swept away by the wind and leaving no trace.

History is ruled by another king,
And a time will come like never before
With His kingdom established upon this earth
King Jesus will reign for evermore.

Tour of the British Museum

This poem was written following a short tour of the British Museum in 2014. Professor Dawkins is one of a large number of people who challenge the authenticity of the Bible, so this tour linking history with the Bible was very encouraging.

The first exhibit we looked at was the Black Obelisk erected in 852 B.C. depicting King Shalmaneser's many conquests. It was found in Assyria in 1846 confirming the Old Testament story of the defeat of Jehu king of Northern Israel, even giving details of the tribute he bought.

Still in the Assyrian section we looked at the Reliefs showing the Assyrian army led by King Sennacherib utterly destroying Lachish in 701 B.C. which was the second most important city in Israel and close to Jerusalem. Sennacherib then sent a deputation to King Hezekiah in Jerusalem telling him he was about to destroy the city. In answer to Hezekiah's prayer, the prophet Isaiah prophesied that the city would be saved, Sennacherib would retreat and not an arrow would be fired on the city. (Read 2 Kings Chapter 19). This in fact happened; Sennacherib returned home and was killed by his two sons as he worshipped in the temple of his god.

Historians and sceptics reputed the story of Belshazzar as completely untrue. Records they said of that period between 556 to 539 B.C. showed Nabonidus was king and there was no mention of Belshazzar. It was just historical fiction.

A discovery was then made in 1881 of a cylinder showing Belshazzar as Nabonidus' eldest son. Nabonidus spent much of his time in Arabia due to poor health and Belshazzar ruled in Babylon as Prince Regent in his father's stead. So it was all true after all.

The British Museum

The world likes to think that the Bible is myth
Not rooted in history, so could not be true
The British Museum has proved otherwise
By its many exhibits – these are just a few.

The Black Obelisk showed Jehu the king
Offering tribute and bowing the knee,
Inscribed on limestone that could not lie
Such evidence was plain to see.

Lachish' destruction was carved on the walls
With Jerusalem next as his fury unfurled,
But Sennacherib left without striking a blow,
Not at arrow was fired as the Bible foretold.

Belshazzar they said was never recorded
That history proved there was no such one,
Nabonidus only ruled over the land
Then a cylinder found revealed Bel was his son.

The scoffers may come and the scoffers may go,
But as hard as they try they always will fail
For time and again new discoveries show
That the truth of God's word will always prevail.

God's handwriting

To the top of the mountain Moses is called
As on tablets of stone God's finger writes,
They are given to Moses containing the Law
To show man how he can live aright.

Belshazzar is feasting with all of his court
When a hand appears and writes on the wall,
The writing reveals he's been weighed in the balance
Foretelling this night that his kingdom will fall.

A woman is caught in adultery,
The Master stoops down and writes on the floor,
He tells those who are sinless to throw the first stone
Then forgives her and tells her to sin no more.

God writes again in a book kept in heaven
The names inscribed there solely by grace,
For those written down in the Lamb's Book of Life
Will one day behold their Saviour's face.

Creation/ Fall/ Redemption/ Glory

The Lord God created all things good
And rested on the seventh day,
His last creation Adam and Eve
Was very good in every way.

How Satan loathed that God should love
A creature such as lowly man,
He tempted them to disobey
And then the reign of sin began.

Cut off from God, barred from His sight
But God foresaw that this would be,
And so the Word, the Son of God
Would come to die for you and me

His sacrifice on that cruel cross
Was made to take away our sin
The gates of glory opened wide
So man once more could enter in.

The stranger

The stranger seemed to just appear
As if from nowhere, out of the air,
He knew her name and told her more
Of things that had never been heard before.

Time now had passed, they were ready to leave,
An arduous journey for them lay ahead,
At last they had reached their journey's end
With nowhere to stay, just a sort of a shed.

Together in wonder they looked at the child
They had wrapped in a blanket and laid in a bed
And then they remembered the stranger who called -
It all had happened, just as he said.

The Christmas message

The date was set in heaven above
When love come down upon this earth,
A stable bare, a bed of straw,
The setting for the Saviour's birth.

Shepherds out upon the hillside
'Watching o'er their flocks by night',
When angels telling of a baby
In splendour burst upon their sight

Signs were seen in distant lands
With wise men travelling from afar
Having searched the skies at night
Came following his natal star.

As we hear the Christmas message,
If we think these things are true,
We could come to seek this baby
We could be like wise men too.

John the Baptist

He came as a prophet of the Most High,
Four hundred years and no word had come
God had been silent until the day
Zacharias was told he would have a son.

He named him John, a wilderness man,
Baptising in Jordan awaiting the day
For the Lamb of God to appear on earth,
John had been sent to prepare the way.

The moment came when Jesus appeared
A voice from heaven, a descending dove,
'This is My Son in whom I'm well pleased'
As John baptised the King of Love.

Miracle of miracles, He came as a man,
Leaving the Godhead, embracing the cross
Jesus our Saviour bearing our sin
Redeeming us back to a Paradise lost.

Meals with Jesus

The tax collector had climbed a tree
Trying to see what it was all about
'Come down Zaccheus, I'll eat at your house',
And Zaccheus' life was turned inside out.

Simon the Pharisee invited the Lord
And at the meal a woman came in,
With tears and perfume she anointed his feet
And Jesus responded forgiving her sin.

Breakfast was ready, fish on the coals
They'd toiled all night and were cold and tired,
'Put your nets down again' the Master called
And fish were caught on the other side.

And now we come to the feast of all feasts,
The Marriage Supper of the Lamb,
Hallelujahs resound over victories won
As we celebrate with the great I Am.

The water of life

She came to the well around midday,
To avoid all the gossip she came alone,
She met a Man there who told her all things
Five husbands she had and one not her own.

He asked for a drink and they started to talk,
A Samaritan woman there with a Jew
Breaking all barriers to meet her need
He told her how she could be made new.

The water of life that He would give
Would mean that she never would thirst again
This transforming draught He offers to all
Once tasted you never will be the same.

At Cana He turned the water to wine
A miracle no one but He could do
Just as the water was wondrously changed
If you drink from this Fount it can happen to you.

(Psalm 34v.8
'O taste and see that the LORD is good')

Thy kingdom come

She wept as she lay the boy on the bier,
First her husband, and now her son.
Life had lost all meaning for her,
She alone was left, all her family gone.

Among the mourners a Man appeared,
He touched the bier and said 'Arise',
The young man sat up at the Master's voice
And the boy was returned to his mother's side.

Who is this who can do such things
Defeating death and the grip of sin?
The One who was promised long ago,
Who came to bring God's kingdom in.

When all the kingdoms on earth have passed,
God's kingdom then will come to birth,
Reversing all that sin has spoiled,
It really will be heaven on earth.

An equestrian tale

He came to Jerusalem on a donkey
Jesus of Nazareth, God's own Word,
They threw down palms crying 'Hosanna'
To Him who came in the Name of the Lord.

The Jews rebuked the people's welcome,
Disliking the honour and fuss that was made.
The Lord replied that if no-one responded
The stones themselves would cry out in praise.

Could they not see that the events unfolding
Were prophesied by the saints of old?
That the Lord would come as it was written
To shepherd His flock into the fold.

When He comes again riding a white horse,
Emblazed on His thigh Faithful and True
He will gather His bride from every nation
As all of creation will be made new.

The I am

He walked on water, stilled the storm,
Wherever He went the blessings came,
He touched the leper, bought sight to the blind,
Whoever He met was never the same.

His teaching had never been heard before,
He spoke as one with authority,
They listened enrapt to His every word,
He was not like a scribe or a Pharisee.

He healed on the Sabbath, it upset them all
And then He said the unthinkable thing,
They could hardly believe their ears when He said
'I am the I Am and can forgive man's sin'.

Enough was enough, they plotted His death,
'This blasphemous talk must end' they said,
'Crucify Him and that is the end',
But He proved them all wrong – and He rose from the dead.

The crossroad

The road was hard, no turning back
The way ordained by mighty God,
'Your will not mine' was all He said
As humbly down that path He trod.

The crowd that cheered Him once with palms
Began to shout for him to die,
They chose Barabbas in his stead
And with one voice cried 'Crucify!'

Between two thieves on Calvary's hill
They put to death the Prince of Life,
One cried for help, the other cursed
The first was promised Paradise.

This promise now is for us all
Christ gave his life to set us free,
The cross divides, it always will -
The question is : what side are we?

The travellers

They travelled together sad and forlorn
With all of their dreams shattered and torn,
It started so well, their hopes were high
Never to guess that He would die.

The Man joined the two as they walked along,
He asked why their faces were sad and long,
'Have you not heard' disbelieving they cried
'How the One we followed was crucified?'

Opening the scriptures He began to unfold
How the Christ should suffer as written of old,
It was not a disaster, but all of God's plan
That one should come as Redeemer of man.

They listened enraptured as slowly they saw
The purpose of God revealed in the Law
The Prophets and Psalms, it's all about Him
The One who should come and rescue from sin.

O that eyes should be opened and scripture made plain,
To see Christ in its pages again and again,
That just like the travellers I too should see
The Master, the Saviour dying for me.

Prove it

Prove it they cried that you're the Messiah
Wouldn't He come as a conquering king?
Not as a poor man riding a donkey
How do you think we'd believe such a thing?

Wherever He went large crowds would follow,
He calmed the storm and turned water to wine,
The lame could walk and the deaf made to hear,
Fully a man and yet also divine.

His teaching had never been heard before,
He fed the five thousand with fish and bread
Gave sight to the blind and lepers were healed,
He cast out demons and raised the dead.

He died on a cross to take away sin
Rose up from the grave, what more could He do
To prove of his love for all of mankind?
Believe it or not – it's all up to you.

Paul the man of God

Holding the clothes while Stephen was stoned
Breathing out fire and filled with hate,
Determined to stamp out the Christian message
Imprisoning all he found in his wake.

Thrown to the ground on the way to Damascus,
A voice from heaven and Paul was made blind
'Who are you Lord?' the reply was given
'I Am Jesus the one that you have denied'.

He was sent to the Gentiles to open their eyes,
To turn them from darkness into the light,
God's plan was to graft them into the vine
Which Paul then embraced with all his might.

Shipwrecked and beaten and left for dead,
He never abandoned the path he trod,
Faithful in all until the end
We're so grateful for Paul the man of God.

Name above all names

Name above all Names, what's in a name?
Jesus, Messiah, He's coming again,
Alpha, Omega, Beginning and End,
Apostle and High Priest, the sinners Friend.

Walking on water, calming the storm,
God incarnate calling us home
Creator, the I Am, nailed to a tree
Lion of Judah dying for me.

Risen, the Victor, conquering King
Coming with clouds redemption to bring
To gather His bride for heaven above
To reign with the Lamb whose name is Love.

The Reformation

The light had dawned, now Luther saw
That all his works would count for nought,
Indulgences could never sway God
Or make him fit for Heaven's court.

Such realization changed his life,
And Martin now saw things anew,
Only by grace could he be saved
And not by anything he could do.

It was the Son's redeeming death
That paid the price for sin in full,
Not by works that any should boast,
And not by any Papal Bull.

Such is the wonder of salvation
When the Father from above,
Poured out his peace and grace upon us
And kissed our guilty world in love.

(500 years ago on 31 October 1517 Martin Luther nailed his famous 95 Thesis on the Castle Church door in Wittenberg.)

We remember

The Somme, Dunkirk and Passchendaele
Cause us to think of times of war,
When men and boys went bravely out
They fought, some died and returned no more.

They gave their all that we should live,
We never should forget such cost,
Remembering with thankful hearts
Our freedom gained as lives were lost.

Another Man gave up his life,
Another war, another fight,
With all mankind held fast in chains
As darkness fell as black as night.

The cost was high, a sinless life
To break the chains and set us free,
The Lamb of God on Calvary's cross
Paid that price for you, for me.

But who do you say I am?

A teacher, a good man, a story teller
All of these things people will say,
A prophet who spoke of heavenly things
But upsetting the religious men of His day?

He healed so many, raised the dead
Easy to see how these tales would grow,
Walking on water, stilling the storm?
These are just stories of long ago!

He loved little children, was friend of the sinner,
So many kindnesses He would do,
And then He said He was one with the Father,
Delusions of grandeur, this could not be true.

He said He would die and rise again,
He said He had come to seek the lost,
He'd come from the Glory and was going home,
This sounds like a mad man – or else He is God!

Ring out the bells

Ring out the bells and let them tell
The wondrous news throughout the land
How Christ was born in Bethlehem
And brought salvation down to man.

God's wisdom had confounded all
Who could have thought of such a plan
As Deity descended low
God's Son encompassed in a span.

He tabernacled here with us,
As God He laid His glory by
He lived as man to bear our sin,
And though a king was crucified.

And can it be He came for us
To take our sin, not just in part?
If this be true, come celebrate
And let the bells ring in our hearts!

Acknowledgements

My thanks go to Anne Coombes, Editor of Parish Pump the Christian website, who has encouraged and commissioned me to write poetry and has been a great source of support.

Thanks also to All Souls Church, Langham Place, London W.1 who week by week faithfully preach the Word of God, and for Rico Tice, Senior Minister, for his encouragement.

I am also grateful to members of the Phrase Writers Group who greatly encouraged me and gave me practical help as I began to express my faith through the medium of poetry.

However, this small book would probably never have been written without the constant help and encouragement of my patient husband Ken, who made me think it was worth putting into print.

But most of all, my eternal thanks are to God himself, who reached down and put my feet upon a rock and gave me not only hope, but a future beyond all my imaginings.

Megan

Megan Carter has been a Christian for many years and came to faith following a family tragedy. Like so many before her, she in desperation cried out to a God in whom she did not believe. Such is the grace of God that over a period of time He revealed Himself to her and no one was more surprised than she was.

She was given a King James Bible by a Christian neighbour and told to read it – which she was desperate enough to do.

From those early beginnings sprang an understanding and amazement at seeing the heart of God that longs for all to be saved and come to a knowledge of His love.

Having always been fond of literature, Megan then began to write short poems, with the hope that they would in some way impart the wonder and majesty of the God she had found, who reveals Himself through His Word.

www.ingramcontent.com/pod-product-compliance
Lightning Source LLC
LaVergne TN
LVHW051713080426
835511LV00017B/2887